Dear Jr.

A blessed Christmas will Jesus Mary and St. Joseph to grant you peace, love, and Joy.

Allow Jesus to Love You

love, Fr. Ralph xo

BARBARA D. ARBUCKLE

Nihil Obstat: Rev. Robert A. Pesarchick
                    Censor Librorum
                    July 17, 2018

Imprimatur: + Most Rev. Charles J. Chaput, O.F.M. Cap.
                    Archbishop of Philadelphia
                    July 19, 2018

Cover image: *Sacred Heart IV* by Charles Bosseron Chambers

Cover design: Rosemary Strohm

Printed in the United States of America
ISBN 978-1-7923-4363-6

DEDICATION

**"I will praise you, Lord, with all my heart;
I will declare all your wondrous deeds."**

—Psalms 9:1

*This book is dedicated to Jesus,
who is my strength and my hope.*

CONTENTS

Entry of Christ Into Jerusalem (engraving) by Julius Schnorr von Carolsfeld

INTRODUCTION

Divine Mercy by Eugeniusz Kazimirowski used with permission of the Marian Fathers of the Immaculate Conception of the B.V.M.

Who is Jesus? Was He simply a holy man who lived a long time ago and performed miracles? Or is He the son of God who can take us to heaven?

We have a free will and can chose to believe whatever we want. There is a spiritual battle going on every day for our souls. Good and evil are at odds with one another.

I chose to believe that Jesus is the light of the world and is our strength. Please give me the opportunity to share with you why I believe this.

My hope is that you will allow Jesus to love you. He only asks you to believe and open the door of your heart!

CHAPTER 1

THINK BEFORE YOU CHOOSE

Saint Teresa of Calcutta

God gave us a free will. We make choices every day of our lives. Every choice has consequences, some good, and others bad. To believe in God is a choice. To love or to hate is a choice. To end your life or the life of another is a choice. History paints a clear picture of what hate in one heart can do. Civilizations can be destroyed and suffer the anguish of war, poverty and starvation.

The choice to love another can also change the lives of many. St. Teresa of Calcutta (Mother Teresa) chose to love, and the rippling effect was felt worldwide.

There really is no better example than our Lord and Savior Jesus Christ. He chose to love the unlovable, forgive the unforgivable and die on a cross even when He knew the suffering would be beyond human comprehension.

When I think of Mary, who is the mother of Jesus and full of grace, I find such peace, comfort and joy. I turn to her with all my worries, and ask her to intercede for my needs and the needs of others. She was chosen above all women to be the mother of our Savior. God created her and knew her heart and soul. She is pure and the most treasured vessel to teach us how to love.

Her "yes" to become the mother of Jesus changed the world. It was never the same from that precious moment on. What a choice Mary made!

Did Mary always know what was next in her life? No, she often pondered and thought before she chose. She was obedient to what God was calling her to.

Mary knew that suffering was part of her life, as well as the joy she experienced. How could a mother choose to stand at the foot of the cross while her son was crucified? She chose to believe that God had a plan. The plan was to trust and be obedient.

Why do people have such a hard time trusting in God? Why is God rarely mentioned on television and in social media? Many people are laughed at for publicly mentioning the word "God." Whom do we trust? What do we believe? Who can we turn to when we are not sure what to do? Who comforts us when tragedy strikes?

A friend may listen and tell you which way to turn and direct your next move. Do they really know what is best for you? Do they really care?

There are plenty of psychiatrists, counselors and therapists to help you along the way. How do you determine which one thinks like you and knows of your deepest needs? Do they really care?

Do our families know us? Many times, the family is the greatest and strongest support when facing a major decision.

Families are generally there for us because we *are* family, and that in itself means so much. It is a blessing to have a family. Of course, there are families that fight one another and are the cause of much distress and pain.

Many times, I have heard that a family who prays together stays together. I have found this to be true in many cases. It is a bond of hope and strength.

Choices are what make a person who they are. Think about those serving in the military, or as police officers and fire fighters. The choices they make in one instant can change their lives forever. They are willing to give their life for another. They thought about this before they took their jobs.

You know the pain of hearing about a school shooting or a terrorist attack. Your heart stops and you listen with such compassion. We are all the same unless your heart has been so hardened as to not feel for others. What happens when someone makes the choice to encounter the shooter? We breathe again, and thank God that no one else had to die.

When a medical team is called in to rescue the injured, we are so grateful. Everyday people help one another, and those choices change lives. We cheer them on, and hope to make a difference ourselves.

There are, and always will be, the poor, the disabled and marginalized people around us. When we see those who serve, clothe and feed them, we know they are doing the Lord's work. They chose this, and usually tell you that it has helped them more than the ones they served.

People are made in the image of God, and reach their greatest joy when they can be used to help someone else.

Our world is full of people who choose to care for our environment. God gave us a beautiful world. He intended us to make good choices. We all seek out clean water, and realize it is a basic necessity to live. We are thankful that people care enough to make a difference in our world.

Look at the love our animals and pets give to us, and the response from their owners. People choose to find loving homes for animals and many times treat them like family members.

Choices can bring us peace, or they can make us miserable and cause much pain and suffering. It is crucial to have someone to go to in order to discern the right choice. Peace is what we all seek.

Choices can be life changing. Reflect on the fact that priests, sisters and missionaries pray intensely, and ponder in their hearts the choice to give their lives to God. Their choice is to give glory to God by serving the needs of others.

I go back to Jesus as the best example for us to turn to. He chose love and peace. He waits patiently for us to allow Him to love us.

His mother, Mary, prays for us and intercedes for us, since she knows the state of our world and the need to make choices that purify our souls.

I recently completed my eighteen-month grand jury duty commitment. It was only one Thursday per month, but it was enough time for me to realize that our choices make all the difference.

I will not disclose any personal information; I just learned that people can make some pretty bad choices. It does not mean that you have to be poor or rich, or of any particular race. You could have been brought up in the best schools, gone to church and have been a highly respected citizen.

Our hearts are what we are full of. What do we feed into our hearts? Is it a desire for power, money and fame?

I do not want to imagine the pain Hitler and Stalin caused in their day and time.

When I listened to the crimes that people committed for money, it crushed me. Was it to buy cars, boats, trips or whatever they desired? Did they ever think about the family members who lost their loved ones due to drug overdoses? There is so much pain and suffering for a lifetime caused by one, or a few, bad choices. There surely is a rippling effect.

"What profit would there be for one to gain the whole world and forfeit his life?"

—Matthew 16:26

I asked one of the detectives what went wrong. I mentioned that I was a kindergarten teacher, and saw the precious innocent faces of many young people. What caused someone to become this way? It came down to making poor choices.

When I heard about a class at our church describing the seven deadly sins and the seven lively virtues, I signed up. See if you recognize how these choices affect your life. I know they affect mine.

Pride/Humility

Envy/Admiration

Anger/Forgiveness

Sloth/Zeal

Avarice (greed)/Generosity

Gluttony/Asceticism (self-denial)

Lust/Chastity

Please know that I, along with you, struggle with these. We are only human and need help. It is only by the grace of God that good overcomes evil.

Our church had a speaker who profoundly affected me, and her name is Immaculée Ilibagiza. I heard her story on the *60 Minutes* broadcast years ago. Rwanda was a country divided by ethnic hatred, and experienced one of the bloodiest genocides in history. Immaculée was in hiding for three months in a tiny bathroom with six other women. She was hunted down following the brutal killing of her family members and many others. She survived, and has dedicated her life to spreading God's message of love and mercy. His call for us is to trust in Him and forgive those who hurt us. The choice is ours.

Thirteen years before the 1994 genocide, the Virgin Mary and Jesus appeared to eight young students in the village of Kibeho, Rwanda. Mary and Jesus warned of "a river of blood," unless Rwandans opened their hearts to God and embraced His love. This did not happen, and the choices were made and the consequences occurred. The people did not listen and turn to God. The consequences were devastating, to say the least. Millions died and hatred ruled in their hearts.

Immaculée has a great devotion to our Blessed Mother, and when she spoke at our church, she held a rosary in her hand while speaking. She wanted us to know the power of this means of prayer. It gave her strength while she was hiding from the vicious murderers. It gives her hope for a world without hatred. Why do people all around the world pray the rosary and find strength and comfort? It is a gift to the world. When our Blessed Mother appeared in Kibeho, she urged all of God's children to pray the rosary daily. Our Blessed Mother was chosen by God to be the Mother of our Savior, Jesus. Let us ask our Blessed Mother to help us make choices that are pleasing to God.

Immaculate Heart V by Charles Bosseron Chambers

Reflection:

*What conscious choice did you make and
what were the consequences?*

CHAPTER 2

WE HAVE A FATHER

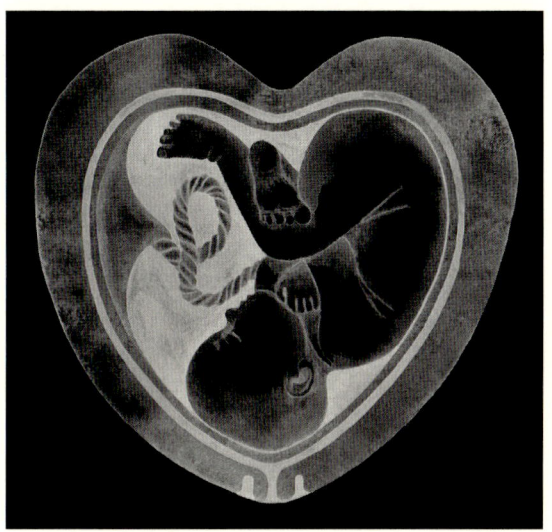

**"See what love the Father has bestowed on us
that we may be called children of God."**

—1 John 3:1

What does it mean to be called children of God? It means that we all
have a heavenly Father who created us out of love, for love and to
share love. He is the same Father for us all. He is for everyone who
ever lived, is alive now and yet to come. This is not determined by
race, creed or color. Everyone is included. How can I state this? I
will refer to the sacred word of God.

"Before I formed you in the womb, I knew you."

—Jeremiah 1:5

Reflect on the miracle of you. There is no one in the world just like you. You are unique and one of a kind. There never was a person like you, and there will never be another you. That is worth thinking about.

Technology is so advanced that fingerprints can determine individual identification. Vast amounts of information can be obtained by your blood sample.

Think about the fact that we are born with only two eyes, one nose and one mouth. Our Father made us each so different and precious in His eyes. Faces are used for identification throughout the world. Criminals are sometimes found simply by facial recognition or DNA.

I have heard the eyes are the windows of the soul. What do you see when you look into someone else's eyes? Many people find it hard to make eye contact. Why is this? Is there something that we need to keep private? Are we protecting ourselves? My own father used to say that you cannot trust a person if they can't look you in the eye.

What about people who are born blind? They see with their hearts. They can determine a person's kindness by the touch of their hand, the softness in their words, the hugs and feelings they receive.

We are blessed with so many gifts. Do you question how a young child can play the piano as well as a master pianist? How about the mathematical genius?

I marvel at the accomplishments of a human being I know, for whom the doctor stated there was little hope for much of a life. I have known her for years. She has such a loving heart. Her kindness and compassion surpass that of most people I know. That counts for a lot. We notice one another's accomplishments. Kindness is a gift to others.

"Since we have gifts that differ according to the grace given
to us, let us exercise them: if prophecy, in proportion to
the faith; if ministry, in ministering; if one is a teacher, in
teaching; if one exhorts, in exhortation; if one contributes,
in generosity; if one is over others, with diligence;
if one does acts of mercy, with cheerfulness."

—Romans 12:6-8

Our Father is the giver of gifts. We are all His children. We simply
need to ask. It may not be what we expect to receive in return, but
will be for our best.

"Ask and it will be given to you; seek and you will find; knock
and the door will be opened to you. For everyone who asks,
receives; and the one who seeks finds; and the one who
knocks the door will be opened. Which one of you would
hand his son a stone when he asks for a loaf of bread or a
snake when he asks for a fish? If you know how to give good
gifts to your children, how much more will your heavenly
Father give good things to those who ask him."

— Matthew 7:7-11

Thousands of years ago, our Father gave Moses the Ten
Commandments. He knew they were needed then, as well as for
the present day.

The Ten Commandments

1. I am the Lord your God: you shall not have strange gods before me.

2. You shall not take the name of the Lord your God in vain.

3. Remember to keep holy the Lord's Day.

4. Honor your father and your mother.

5. You shall not kill.

6. You shall not commit adultery.

7. You shall not steal.

8. You shall not bear false witness against your neighbor.

9. You shall not covet your neighbor's wife.

10. You shall not covet your neighbor's goods.

"For I know well the plans I have in mind for you- plans for your welfare and not for woe, so as to give you a future of hope. When you call me, and come and pray to me, I will listen to you. When you look for me, you will find me. Yes, when you seek me with all your heart."

—Jeremiah 29: 11-14

Reflection:

Can you believe that you have a heavenly Father who loves you and knows what is best for you?

CHAPTER 3
JESUS

Christ's Image by Heinrich Hofmann

Jesus is the most recognized name in the entire world. People contemplate who Jesus is, and for many, it is a lifelong quest. My journey with Jesus has grown and is still growing.

I have collected holy cards since I was a little girl. Recently, I came across one with a picture of Jesus who was suffering with a crown of thorns placed on His head. When I read the back of the card, I was moved by the following words:

One Life

*He was born in a stable, in an obscure village,
from there He traveled, less than 200 miles.*

*He never won an election, He never went to college, He never owned
a home, He never had a lot of money.*

*He became a nomadic preacher, popular opinion turned against Him,
He was betrayed by a close friend, and His other friends ran away.*

*He was unjustly condemned to death, crucified on a cross
among common thieves, on a hill overlooking the town dump,
and when dead, laid in a borrowed grave.*

*Nineteen centuries have come and gone, Empires have risen and fallen,
mighty armies have marched, and powerful rulers have reigned.*

*Yet no one has affected men as much as He, He is the central figure of
the human race, He is the Messiah, the Son of God, JESUS CHRIST.*

As a child, I believed Jesus was the precious baby born of Mary and
Joseph. I went to a Catholic grade school, so I knew that Jesus was
the one who changed everything. He brought peace to our world,
loved all people and gave His life up so we could all go to heaven
and be with Him there.

It was a simple message and not complicated. It filled me with a peace
that words cannot express. Funny thing is, now I am almost seventy
years old and it still fills me with a peace that words cannot express.

As I grew, I questioned where Jesus is in this crazy and self-centered
world. I forgot to look for Him. I got busy and had a life to live.

When I was in high school, I took secretarial classes since I had
no intention of going to college. But I had a strong desire to know
God in a personal way. I felt that I was being called to teach young
children about God.

When I asked my guidance counselor about attending a college, he, in no uncertain terms, let me know that no college would accept me. I did not have college prep classes. I was very disappointed. Not long after hearing this, I was called to his office. He found a junior college that would accept me as a three-year student instead of in their two-year program. Needless to say, I was thrilled.

I did not understand at the time that God was guiding all of the experiences that were to come. The school was next to an orphanage, where I loved spending time and meeting the young children. I was expected to experience many social situations that began to open my heart to the needs of others, especially those suffering. I remember a home nearby that housed children with various health conditions that prevented them from living in their own homes. It was painful for me to even hear about, but suffering for anyone is usually not welcomed. I never knew such heartaches existed.

I had the opportunity to fill water pitchers at the Hospital of the University of Pennsylvania. Even if I did not have much personal contact, I knew people were suffering. I visited a home for delinquent girls. I wondered why they had made the choices that caused such sadness.

I visited a home for the mentally ill. It has since closed, but I will never forget the anguish I felt for people who were tortured and lost. Their torture was not for me to understand, but to just feel their pain and their isolation was enough. I felt the pain of those who cared for them. I remember leaving the group and running to the school bus to hide from the fear and pain that I was feeling. How could people go there each and every day and fear for their lives? I recall many people moaning, and one person jumped at me. Some patients were adults left in cribs for life. No wonder the institution closed. Compassionate people must have seen the need for a change. My hope is that someone cares for these people and loves them.

An experience which brought great joy was helping in a classroom of underprivileged children. Simple joys were hearing the laughter, and seeing them appreciate anything they received and the way they thought of one another, even when they didn't have much themselves.

These experiences were gifts from God that opened my heart to humanity.

I moved on to West Chester University, and graduated with a degree in early childhood education. Teaching jobs were few. I married my high school sweetheart and had two amazing children. Now I am blessed with three grandsons. I could never express how much love and joy I receive from my family.

On my journey of faith, I taught full-day kindergarten for sixteen years in a Catholic school. I had always wanted to teach in a Catholic school so that I could tell the children how much God loves them. It is a beautiful way to start each day in prayer. It is powerful to hear the children's prayers, and they are so simple and pure. It was just part of our everyday life.

My younger sister, Susan, wanted me to experience Jesus in a personal way, and introduced me to Wayne Monbleau. I listened to his tapes and heard him speak in person. This guided me along the path of knowing that Jesus was not just a faraway figure, but someone who loved me even with all my imperfections.

I have taken many Bible studies, and have a great desire to read about Jesus and learn from Him. I hunger to hear how He healed, forgave, comforted, brought peace, loved the unlovable, taught His apostles by His actions, showed compassion and was full of kindness. I wanted this.

At the heart of Jesus's teachings are the Beatitudes.

> **"Blessed are the poor in spirit, for theirs
> is the kingdom of heaven.**
>
> **Blessed are they who mourn, for they will be comforted.**
>
> **Blessed are the meek, for they will inherit the land.**
>
> **Blessed are they who hunger and thirst for righteousness,
> for they will be satisfied.**
>
> **Blessed are the merciful, for they will be shown mercy.**
>
> **Blessed are the clean of heart, for they will see God.**
>
> **Blessed are the peacemakers, for they will be
> called children of God.**
>
> **Blessed are they who are persecuted for the sake of
> righteousness, for theirs is the kingdom of heaven."**
>
> **—Matthew 5:3-10**

While teaching in a Catholic school, I was blessed to work alongside the IHM Sisters (Sisters, Servants of the Immaculate Heart of Mary). They are special women in many ways. They give their lives to Jesus and model their lives after Mary, the mother of Jesus.

When I first started teaching, I recall a gathering of people outside my classroom at the end of a busy day. I joined in and was told that one of the sisters in her twenties had just passed from breast cancer. I told one of the sisters that I was sorry to hear this, and especially because she was so young. She corrected me and told me not to be sorry. She let me know that sister had now received her eternal reward. I later thought of what she said. Yes, she gave her life to Jesus and was now receiving her eternal reward. That is a simple message and I understood.

Did you ever have a dream that had a clear message for you? I did.

I dreamed that Sister Edwardine was looking for a nightgown for her friend and was having a hard time. I offered to help her. Sister Edwardine and I used to work together. She had a great sense of humor and loved to joke. When I saw her in the hallway before the children entered school, I told her of my dream. She froze and stared at me. I thought she would make a joke about what I had just told her. Instead, I froze from her response to me.

She told me that nuns do not usually spend the day at the mall, but she had just done so. She was trying to find a nightgown for her friend. Her friend had just had a stroke and was paralyzed on one side. The nightgown needed to be extra-large for her to move in.

Immediately I asked, who is your friend and what size nightgown are you looking for? She gave me the information, and I told her I would find two nightgowns and meet her friend. She told me her friend's name was Sister Kateri, and she lived at Camilla Hall.

We both knew this was all a message from God. So, off I went to the mall and purchased two extra-large nightgowns. When I introduced myself and told Sister Kateri why I was there and how this all came about, she giggled and welcomed me as her new friend. God works in mysterious ways and none of us questioned this.

This friendship lasted many years. My mother became a frequent visitor and friend too. Camilla Hall is a special place for retired sisters. My mother was up in years, and loved to share stories with Sister Edwardine and Sister Kateri. My mother found comfort in their compassionate ways and often asked them to pray for her.

The four of us shared years of laughter and remembering our loved ones. We prayed for one another. We knew we were each a gift to one another.

Once I asked a kind and loving aide to help me take the two sisters to Ocean City, New Jersey. They could hardly believe this was going to happen. Sister Kateri was in a wheelchair and needed assistance, but made it to the boardwalk. I still hear their laughter as the two sisters giggled while eating ice cream cones on the Ocean City boardwalk. It was as if they were two little girls just taking in the fun.

When my husband used to wonder what I was doing with the sisters, I would tell him that I was on a mission from God. He has laughed many times, since one of his favorite movies is *The Blues Brothers*. In the movie, Jake and Elwood Blues were determined to save the Catholic orphanage in which they were raised. Their words were, "We're on a mission from God."

I became close to Sister Edwardine and asked many questions. When I mentioned that people think sisters give up so much, she corrected me and told me how much they receive. When Sister retired from teaching, she volunteered in a prison. She let me know how choices made all the difference. People did not think before they chose to take a gun and kill someone. It was impulse.

I learned many lessons within the halls of Camilla Hall. When the sisters came together to fold the community laundry, it was a joy-filled experience and not a chore.

When Sister Edwardine walked down the hallway, you could see how she struggled to walk. She had had polio as a child. She walked with such a purpose and joy to feed another sister who could not feed herself. I never heard her talk about this as a job, but as a loving opportunity.

I remember taking her to Kmart to purchase a piece of equipment for another sister who could not speak. She was probably giving her a tape recorder to hear her loved ones' messages. I can't remember the details, but knew Sister Edwardine was on her own mission.

Sister Kateri and Sister Edwardine were sent to South America as missionaries when they were younger, and they were happy to be together. While they were serving in South America, Sister Edwardine received a phone call that her mother was not expected to live much longer. Sister Edwardine loved her mother dearly, and she told me how hard this was for her. It was Christmastime, and she placed a piece of straw by Jesus in the manger and asked Him to please take her mother soon. A short time later the announcement was made that her mother had passed.

She knew Jesus had come for her mother and this pleased her greatly.

I was with Sister Edwardine days before she passed. She had had a stroke and was not able to speak. When she saw me, her eyes opened wide, and she tried hard to grasp the crucifix on her lap. Every movement was a struggle. I knew what she was telling me without words. I stayed and prayed a rosary and she spoke with her eyes.

When you attend the funeral of a sister and listen to the voices of the other sisters, you can close your eyes and be in heaven.

When my own mother was not expected to live much longer, I asked Baby Jesus in the manger to carry her through the coming days. When I returned home, there happened to be a Christmas card on the table with Jesus carrying a lamb. I believe He does carry us. My mother passed in March. The day before she passed, she could not speak, but reached for a picture of Jesus. People speak and do not need words. We know what their hearts are full of.

Shortly after my mother passed, the book I, along with four other women, worked on, titled *With God's Grace*, was published. It was a blessing to know my mother knew it would be published, since she listened to me talk about it for years.

One of the authors, Sister Janice McGrane, happened to pass three days prior to the book being published. She had told me months before that she was full of cancer and the prognosis was not good.

I remember when she told me that all she wanted was to be with Jesus. I cried and told her I would pray that Jesus would carry her through what she would need to go through.

After she passed, one of the sisters mentioned that they were singing a song about Jesus carrying her in her last moments. Sister Janice then smiled while looking up, and passed.

I find great comfort in my belief that Jesus does come to those who ask for Him.

With hours to write a dedication to Sister Janice before the book's publication, I wrote the following:

> Her life was given to Jesus.
> Her sufferings were tied to Jesus.
> Her connections brought us to Jesus.
> Her writings told of Jesus.
> Her works for the unloved and disabled were for Jesus.
> Her weakened state reached for Jesus.
> Her prayer was to be with Jesus.
> Thank you, Jesus, for taking our beloved friend to heaven.

Sister Janice McGrane, SSJ passed on Monday, June 27, 2016.

It is not just at death that He is there for us. Believe that Jesus walks and talks with us every day. Sometimes it is through other people or an unusual event.

I woke up one morning and heard those words, "He walks with me and He talks with me." I went to the computer and did my research. There is a beautiful song that is sung by many popular artists, titled, "In the Garden." Some of the words are:

> "And He walks with me, and He talks with me,
> And He tells me I am His own;
> And the joy we share as we tarry there
> None other has ever known."

It is a choice to believe in coincidences or not. I choose to believe that Jesus really cares about us and walks with us through this journey of life. We are not alone, especially in the dark times of life. This happened again to me; I woke up and heard the words and melody of "Be Not Afraid." I knew this song from church.

Some of the words are:

> "Be not afraid.
> I go before you always.
> Come follow me,
> And I will give you rest."

Like you, I have had those dark times. We can all be comforted to hear: be not afraid.

"Have no anxiety at all, but in everything by prayer and petition with thanksgiving make your requests known to God. Then the peace of God that surpasses all understanding will guard your hearts and minds in Christ Jesus."

—Philippians 4:6-7

Reflection:

Who do you say Jesus is?

CHAPTER 4
COME HOLY SPIRIT

Jesus speaks to His disciples:

"I have told you this while I am with you. The Advocate, the Holy Spirit that the Father will send in my name—he will teach you everything and remind you of all that I told you. Peace I leave with you; my peace I give to you. Not as the world gives do I give it to you. Do not let your hearts be troubled or afraid.

You heard me tell you, I am going away and I will come back to you. If you loved me, you would rejoice that I am going to the Father; for the Father is greater than I."

—John 14:25-28

It is best to use scripture to explain the coming of the Spirit. Jesus came to His disciples following His resurrection. He came to empower them with the Holy Spirit. This prepared them to witness to all the nations.

"When the time for Pentecost was fulfilled, they were all in one place together. And suddenly there came from the sky a noise like a strong driving wind, and it filled the entire house in which they were. Then there appeared to them tongues as of fire, which parted and came to rest on each one of them. And they were all filled with the Holy Spirit and began to speak in different tongues, as the Spirit enabled them to proclaim."

—Acts 2:1-4

Have you ever heard someone speak in tongues?

It must have been forty years ago that I first attended a Charismatic Healing Mass. I could not help but raise my arms and sway to the music as people praised God. I felt a little out of sorts since I heard so many different sounds coming from people. I marveled at the whole experience. Why did I need any explanation other than to know that praise is praise?

What does it mean to live by the Spirit?

"I say, then: live by the Spirit and you will certainly not gratify the desire of the flesh. For the flesh has desires against the Spirit, and the Spirit against the flesh; these are opposed to each other, so that you may not do what you want."

—Galatians 5:16-17

When you look at the world and the way most people live, you have to say it is mostly by the flesh. It is hard to live in this present time and not be caught up in all its trappings. Television, internet and social media are our main connections to one another. We know immediately what is happening around the world. We are surely connected. But what are we connected to?

Many of us define ourselves by our friends, education, social status, homes, cars, and how we socialize. How do we socialize? Drinking is a big part of our gatherings. It has caused a lot of problems, too. Once we drink, it is not always easy to determine how much is too much. Our state of mind changes, we become more passionate and choices are affected.

Drugs are also an option in our world. When you watch television, you can hear about a drug for almost anything. Many drugs can be helpful, but many are at the core of abuse, death and suicide. Our country is in a very bad state at this time with the abuse of drugs. When you know of someone who has lost their life from a drug overdose, you know the pain of the family is beyond description.

As I share the following scripture, you be the judge about how our culture lives. Are we living more in the flesh, or in the Spirit?

**"Now the works of the flesh are obvious: immorality, impurity, licentiousness, idolatry, sorcery, hatreds, rivalry, jealously, outbursts of fury, acts of selfishness, dissensions, factions, occasions of envy, drinking bouts, orgies and the like.
I warn you, as I warned you before, that those who do such things will not inherit the kingdom of God.
In contrast, the fruit of the Spirit is love, joy, peace, patience, kindness, generosity, faithfulness, gentleness, self-control. Against such there is no law. Now those who belong to Jesus have crucified their flesh with its passions and desires."**

Galatians 5:19-24

The evil needs no explanation. I choose to focus on living in the Spirit and the fruits it produces. I took some of the fruits and defined my interpretation. I hope you will do the same.

LOVE

"You shall love the Lord, your God, with all your heart, with all your being, with all your strength, and with all your mind, and your neighbor as yourself."

Luke 10:27

I was blessed to know I was loved by my parents, the Sisters of Saint Joseph at the elementary school I attended, and by the kind people who nurtured me along in my youth.

My husband and I went together in high school, fell in love, went to the prom, rode on his motorcycle, became hippies, shared the pains of growing up in a crazy world, spent time apart, found each other, got married, had children and had grandchildren. We are happily married now for forty-seven years. When we look at all that happened, all that really mattered is that we loved.

Love does not always end in marriage; that is not the point. It is celebrating the love with the people God has placed in your life.

**"So faith, hope, love remain, these three,
but the greatest of these is love."**

1 Corinthians 13:13

JOY

A religious sister once told me that true joy is when you put Jesus first, then others, then yourself.

Jesus, others, yourself (in that order).

I find joy in knowing Jesus is always with me and trying to bring Him to others. I find joy in my family; in the laughter we share and in helping someone else. That joy is in the simple things of life. When I was younger, I did some needlework. I recall one saying had the following words: "To love and be loved is the greatest joy on earth."

PEACE

"Have the same regard for one another; do not be haughty but associate with the lowly; do not be wise in your own estimation. Do not repay anyone evil for evil; be concerned for what is noble in the sight of all. If possible, on your part, live at peace with all."

Romans 12:16-18

Just imagine for a moment how different the world would be if we really took care of the lowly or those in need? It would be wonderful to listen to one another, and not believe we alone have all the answers. Instead of fighting evil with evil, we could make better choices. It is only a dream, but a beautiful dream to imagine that we all treat one another with respect and live in peace. I used to have a peace prayer for my kindergarten students posted in the classroom. It stated, "Let peace begin with me."

KINDNESS

My heart was warmed as I listened to an Amish girl tell me of her trip to Mexico. She was my waitress. She rode on a bus for fifty hours. She, along with others, helped to build three homes for those in need. She was so full of joy telling me how a single mother with cancer, having six children, would now have a home to live in. It is the kindness that warms a heart!

GENEROSITY

When I think of generosity, I think of God's mercy. A young polish nun teaches us a lot about God's mercy. Her name is St. Faustina. Jesus appeared to her, and told her how He wanted the world to know of His mercy. He showed her an image of Jesus pouring out His love for us. This image is placed in most churches around the world. I placed this image at the entrance of our home. I look at the image of Jesus throughout the day, and think how Jesus wants us to come to Him with everything. Everything means with all our joys and sorrows, all our worries and fears. He is full of mercy and love. He just wants us to trust in Him.

Jesus's words from St. Faustina's Diary #570

"By means of this image I shall be granting many graces to souls; so, let every soul have access to it."

We are all in need of God's generous mercy. He asked His heavenly

Father to forgive those who tortured and crucified Him. He wants us to forgive one another.

"Be merciful, just as your Father is merciful."

—Luke 6:36

FAITHFULNESS

As a child, my faith was strong, although as I grew, I questioned where God is. I remember asking my Nan (my father's mother) "Do you think there is a God?"

She replied, "Yes, and don't ask that question again."

I talked freely with Nan about many concerns that I had. But she did not want to talk about religion. She did have a picture of Jesus as the Good Shepherd over her bed. She was full of compassion, and always looked out for those in need.

On the other hand, I had my Bubba (my mother's mom). She was the most loving person that I have ever met. She usually had a rosary in her hand and prayed a lot. She lived with my grandfather and seven children in a small house in the back of an alley. I grew up quite comfortably, and never in need of anything. Visiting my grandparents was quite an experience for me, so whenever I went to visit, I observed the differences. My mother had a strong faith, so this was not different. It was the conditions in which they lived. The house had four rooms and was filled with people and laughter. When we attended a pilgrimage in the mountains outside of Pittsburgh, I watched the kneeling, praying and devotion of many people. It is the beauty of a soul that stands out. It is not words, but actions, that make you notice. It was her faith. The faith of my two grandmothers is not for me to judge. They were both amazing models for me. I believe God looks upon the heart.

GENTLENESS

There is a very tender picture of Jesus holding a baby lamb. He is holding the lamb close to His neck, and the image to me is gentleness. It is a loving embrace and brings to mind Jesus as the Good Shepherd.

"I am the good shepherd. A good shepherd lays down his life for the sheep. A hired man, who is not a shepherd and whose sheep are not his own, sees a wolf coming and leaves the sheep and runs away, and the wolf catches and scatters them. This is because he works for pay and has no concern for the sheep. I am the good shepherd, and I know mine and mine know me, just as the Father knows me and I know the Father and I will lay down my life for the sheep."

John 10:11-15

SELF-CONTROL

"Every athlete exercises discipline in every way. They do it to win a perishable crown, but we an imperishable one."

—1 Corinthians 9:25

I may have been ten years old when I attended my first Philadelphia Eagles football game. It was loud, rowdy, with lots of drunken men screaming, and not for me. My father's office was near the stadium, so he was able to walk to the stadium. My father became a true Eagles fan. I frequently heard the yelling from my father and brother. Then, after I got married, my husband and son became great fans. My husband was so loud that I told people it was like having a one-man party going on when he watched the game. I watched very few games in my life and still do not understand the game. What drew my attention was when Carson Wentz was being interviewed. I heard words that came from praising God. He was not afraid to let others know that God was first in his life. This is highly unusual, and I wanted to hear more. Then, after Carson Wentz was injured, Nick

Foles took his place as the Eagles quarterback. He was interviewed after winning the NFC Championship. The first thing that came out of his mouth was, "All glory to God." Wow, I was won over.

When Eagles Coach Doug Pederson was asked how it feels to go from being a high school coach to a Super Bowl coach, he let the public know that it is because he is rooted and grounded in his savior, Jesus Christ. Well, at this point, you could have picked me up off the floor.

I was so impressed that the glory was given to God and that someone with such a standing could publicly say his savior is Jesus Christ. Our world has gotten so self-centered, with people seeking credit for all the accomplishments. It is so refreshing to have people, athletes or not, give glory to God and our Lord and Savior, Jesus Christ. These men showed many others that the real crown of winning is not a perishable one.

Reflection:

How have you been blessed by the fruits of the Holy Spirit?

CHAPTER 5
GRACE IS A GIFT FROM GOD

"My grace is sufficient for you, for power is made perfect in weakness."

—2 Corinthians 12:9

This is one of the most powerful messages in Scripture, if you allow it.

God can work in and through us when we give ourselves to Him. I do not speak of weakness as a bad thing. It is when we are humble that He can do His greatest work. He will be our strength, if we allow it.

I was blessed to experience God's healing grace at a difficult time in my life. Life became overwhelming and I had experienced panic attacks. I had two ambulance rides to the hospital within one month. I saw a therapist, had the help of my family (especially my sister Gerry), along with many prayers that were said for me.

I surrendered my life to God and received His healing grace. I wanted Him to take over for me and be my strength. I learned many helpful ways to cope with stress that came my way, but my strength comes from Jesus. I wanted others to know that grace is real and a gift from God. I marvel at how God has been the master weaver in the next steps of this journey of life.

Four women came together who did not know one another. We all shared our unique and life-changing experiences of God's grace. We had a book published in 2016.

Grace is a gift, and different for each person. God knows our needs and what is best for us. I will share these women's words of grace with you.

SISTER JANICE MCGRANE, SSJ

"I was thirty-eight years old, a Sister of Saint Joseph, and worked in disability ministry for the Metuchen Diocese of central New Jersey. Also, I had been diagnosed with rheumatoid arthritis twenty years before."

Janice went to Lourdes, France in hopes of a cure.

"I believe that grace is God's way of talking to us, inviting us to grow. An image I have long had portrays God as knocking on the windows of our soul, trying to communicate with us, to gently nudge us in a good direction. I am happy that God nudged me into the grotto upon my arrival at Lourdes, because it was there that I had the first religious experience of my pilgrimage.

The female attendant assisted me into a scanty white robe. Two women then gently lowered me into the bath itself. I was shocked at how cold the water was. I let it swirl around my body for a few moments, praying, hoping earnestly for my own private miracle. Nothing happened. I knew immediately that I was not cured. Indeed, my joints were rather vigorously protesting this unexpected frigid shock treatment. The women assisted me out of the bath. I returned to my wheelchair and pushed out into the sunlit grotto area.

No, I did not receive the grace I so eagerly sought from my pilgrimage to Lourdes. I was not cured.

I was anointed.

As God makes clear '...my thoughts are not your thoughts, nor are your ways my ways...' (Isaiah 55:8).

When I went to Lourdes in 1987, I knew exactly what grace I desired. I wanted to be hale and hearty--to have the inflammatory process that was tearing at my joints stop completely. That didn't happen. Instead, I received a greater grace: I was clear about who I was now, a woman religious working in disability ministry within the church already, but now I knew that God wanted me to speak and advocate for acceptance, accessibility, and, most difficult of all, attitudinal change toward people with disabilities."

ELISA TAYLOR BERRY

"Everything is a grace, an unmerited gift of God's extravagant love for me. I did not always know this because of all the abuse I endured as a child, but I do now.

This extraordinary grace in my life began much earlier though, even before I was born. From my first moments after taking my first breath, in a small third-floor apartment, I was in serious trouble. I was born three months too soon. My mother did not realize she was still pregnant. Several months before, she had gone to a doctor to undo the whole thing. She had an abortion.

After arriving at the hospital, doctors told my parents two things: pick a name for her, and call a priest to have her baptized because she will not survive the day. My father yelled at the doctors and my mother that no one was to name me until he got back. He walked out of the hospital and straight to the nearest bar, where he called my grandmother to ask her to send a priest to the hospital. He sat down at the bar to drink and think of a name. While there, the song Mona Lisa came over the radio. My father jumped up and ran back to the hospital. From that song he came up with the name Elisa.

My name means consecrated to God or House of God. I am sure my father did not know this. God did. I'm thinking God knew someday this knowledge would console me and that, no matter what happened to me, I was to know for certain I belonged to Him. This was the information I would need to hold in my heart at all times... to survive."

Elisa shared the abuse that both of her parents put her through. The remarkable thing is she was able to forgive them, and this is only by the grace of God.

I have been blessed to know Elisa now for many years, and she pours out so much love and forgiveness because she knows how much God loves her and wants others to know the same.

She has touched the lives of many through her prison ministry. She shared the wisdom given to us by Saint Thérèse of Lisieux in the Yellow Notebook:

"Everything is a grace, everything is the direct effect of our Father's love-difficulties, contradictions, humiliations, all the soul's miseries, her burdens, her needs, everything, because through them, she learns humility, realizes her weakness. Everything is a grace because everything is God's gift. Whatever be the character of life or its unexpected events-to the heart that loves, all is well."

ARLENE FINOCCHIARO

"The mist was all around me as I rocked in a little boat at the base of Niagara Falls. The water thundered as it fell from high above. You couldn't see where it was coming from, but it flowed non-stop, delighting the onlookers huddled in their blue plastic ponchos.

Everyone made the choice to relish the experience and be submerged in the spray, or to hide in the middle of the boat and stay dry.

Grace is like that loving mist of God's life ever flowing from the Father, the Son and the Holy Spirit. When we stick our neck out in the mist, it refreshes, guides, cleanses, heals and gives joy when we least expect it. The closer we get to the falls, the wetter we get. If we hold out our buckets, God will fill them to overflowing with His grace.

Always carry an empty bucket. You never know when God will fill it up. Like the waterfall, God's grace is ever-flowing. With your heart and mind open, hold out your bucket. His grace is there for the asking."

"Ask and it will be given to you; seek and you will find; knock and the door will be opened to you. For everyone who asks, receives; and the one who seeks, finds; and to the one who knocks, the door will be opened."

—Matthew 7:7-8

ANNETTE HUG

"I met Mike, who was a pilot and skydiver. I began going with Mike on flights and watching him skydive. Before I knew it, I was no longer content just watching him skydive; I started training to jump. It was thrilling. I loved it.

Skydiving became a new way of life for me, and I stopped attending Mass. I drifted farther and farther away from my faith. With this new life, doubts and frustrations arose. I had a nagging suspicion that there was more to life than just work, friends and fun. Something was missing.

Since Mike was older than me, he wanted the relationship to move along faster and towards marriage. I considered it and accepted his proposal, thinking the commitment to marriage would eradicate this constant void. To my great disappointment, it did little or nothing to replace the deep, dull pain inside my soul. In time, I told him I was not yet ready to make the commitment to marriage. He accepted my postponement and agreed to wait for a later date. The following weekend we went to the drop zone as usual. The only difference was Mike used another kind of parachute in addition to his usual parachute. He wanted to use this parachute for the last jump of the day. That decision turned out to be fatal. On his last jump, Mike's main parachute and his reserve both malfunctioned and he plunged to his death. I watched as he got closer and closer to the ground. I began screaming. "Pull!" Pull!" I saw him trying to hit the parachute to make it open, but it was no use. I was in shock. I had never witnessed such horror in all my life.

My life spiraled out of control. I fell into a deep depression. At twenty, the accident was almost too much to handle. Thankfully, my mother and father were instrumental in helping restore my physical, mental and spiritual health. My skydiver friends shuttled me through the worst part of the tragedy. They were, and still are, true friends. Their faithful presence was a sign of God's grace."

God is always at work ready to pour out His grace. We just need to open our hearts and receive it. I once heard a beautiful image on grace. It is like turning on the water from the spigot. You just need to turn it on and the water flows. It is the same with grace. We will receive it if we are open to receive what is freely and graciously given.

Reflection:

How has God graced your life?

CHAPTER 6
HOW COULD JESUS LOVE ME?

We all wonder about this question. We are all sinners. Jesus came to save us from our sins, not to condemn us.

"For God did not send His Son into the world to condemn the world, but that the world might be saved through Him."

—John 3:17

We may think that we really don't do much wrong. We think how we are not in the same category as murderers and rapists. Keep an open heart as you reflect on someone who murdered and repented. He is also embraced by the love of God.

I was moved by the writings of Elisa (co-author of *With God's Grace*) as she told of her work in prison ministry. She was a retreat volunteer for Kairos Prison Ministry. She prayed beside a serial killer and shared the following:

"God loves each one of us so deeply and intensely without exception. His love is not based on what we have or what we have done. It is because of who we are. We are His BELOVED, every single one of us. Even this serial killer was not outside God's extravagant mercy and love. He also was one of God's precious children. The tears choked back in this man's chest to the point that he could barely speak. I knew he felt Jesus lovingly touch his heart. I was not called to judge this man. I was only called to love him with God's love.

Here is an example of what God's agape love can do in the heart and soul of a participant during their special time with God. During the closing ceremony, a woman got up to speak. Holding back tears, she went on to tell all of us that she would never get out of prison. She knew she would be there until Jesus called her home. She said this with a smile on her face and tears in her eyes. She said that no one would shut her up ever again. She was beaming when she told us that she would spend the rest of her life in prison telling anyone who would listen what she learned on her Kairos journey."

"Stop judging, that you may not be judged. For as you judge, so will you be judged, and the measure with which you measure will be measured out to you. Why do you notice the splinter in your brother's eye, but do not perceive the wooden beam in your own eye? How can you say to your brother, 'Let me remove that splinter from your eye,' while the wooden beam is in your own eye? You hypocrite, remove the wooden beam from your eye first; then you will see clearly to remove the splinter from your brother's eye."

Matthew: 7:1-5

After reading the Parable of the Prodigal Son, I reflected on how I look at myself. The central message was that the younger son took his inheritance and squandered it; he became remorseful, humbled and begged his father for forgiveness. The older brother had a hard time with the celebration that the father gave to his brother. He felt he tried to do everything right, and why should the brother be given a party? The father explained that it is a time for rejoicing when someone returns and regrets his fallen ways.

I know it is hard to understand how we are all forgiven when some of us try to do the right thing, and others make such bad choices. Yet, God sees the heart and wants us all to return to Him. There is a sin of pride. It is so easy to look at others and think, I'm glad that I am not like them.

I will share a reflection from the book titled *The Return of the Prodigal Son* by Henri J.M. Nouwen. It helped me see things as the world sees them, and not as God sees them.

"To whom do I belong—to God, or to the world?

Often, I am like a small boat on the ocean, completely at the mercy of its waves. All the time and energy that I spend keeping some kind of balance and preventing myself from being tipped over and drowning shows that my life is mostly a struggle for survival: it is not a holy struggle, but an anxious struggle, resulting from the mistaken idea that it is the world that defines me. As long as I keep running about asking: 'Do you love me? Do you really love me?' I give all power to the voices of the world and put myself in bondage, because the world is filled with ifs. The world says: 'Yes, I love you if you are good-looking, intelligent, and wealthy. I love you if you have a good education, a good job, and good connections. I love you if you produce much, sell much, and buy much.' There are endless ifs hidden in the world's love. These ifs enslave me, since it is impossible to respond adequately to all of them. The world's love is, and always will be, conditional. As long as I remain hooked to the world, I will be trying, failing, and trying again. It is a world that fosters addictions, because what it offers cannot satisfy the deepest craving of my heart.

God rejoices. Not because the problems of the world have been solved, not because all human pain and suffering have come to an end, nor because thousands of people have converted and are now praising Him for His goodness. No, God rejoices because one of His children who was lost has been found. What I am called to is to enter into that joy. It is God's joy, not the joy that the world offers."

Reflection:

Do you believe Jesus could love you?

CHAPTER 7
BELIEVE IT!

Christ the Consolator by Carl Heinrich Bloch

Believe you are loved! You are unique and precious in the eyes of God. There is only one you, and God made you in His image. You were made in love, for love and to share this love. God knows your every thought, your desires, your worries and your joys.

If you wonder how precious you are, look at the birds, animals, flowers and trees. They were all specially made by God. Yet, we are far more important to God.

"Look at the birds in the sky; they do not sow or reap, they gather nothing into barns, yet your heavenly Father feeds them. Are you not more important than they? Can any of you by worrying add a single moment to your life span? Why are you anxious about clothes? Learn from the way wildflowers grow. They do not work or spin. But I tell you that not even Solomon in all his splendor was clothed like one of them. If God so clothes the grass of the field which grows today and is thrown into the oven tomorrow, will He not much more provide for you, O you of little faith? So do not worry and say 'What are we to eat?' or 'What are we to drink?' or 'What are we to wear?' All these things the Pagans seek. Your heavenly Father knows you need them all. But seek first the Kingdom of God and His righteousness and all these things will be given you besides. So do not worry about tomorrow, tomorrow will take care of itself."

—Matthew 6:26-34

Reflection:

Do you believe that God knows of your deepest concerns? Would you be willing to trust in His love for you?

CHAPTER 8
ALLOW IT!

Suffer the Little Children by Vogel von Vogelstein

When I say "allow it," I am referring to the fact that you have a free will and can allow Jesus to love you, or not.

Many people came to Jesus with questions and hoping for a miracle. I imagine how peaceful it must have been when He left the crowds and prayed in solitude. He often prayed and spoke to His heavenly Father for comfort and strength. What a beautiful example Jesus is for us when we turn to our heavenly Father for comfort and strength.

The disciples discouraged the children from coming too close to Jesus. Many people think children should be removed, since they have little to add to the conversation. We believe they are not mature enough to join in on the conversation.

Jesus had a desire to be with the children. He must have felt such a refreshing change from people questioning His every move. Jesus saw the children in a different light. He called the children to come to Him.

"Amen, I say to you, unless you turn and become like children, you will not enter the kingdom of heaven. Whoever humbles himself like this child is the greatest in the kingdom of heaven."

—Matthew 18: 3-4

There is no better example of humility than Jesus. He came to serve, and not be served. He humbly prayed, healed the suffering, consoled, fed the hungry, forgave sins, brought the dying back to life, wept with His friends, welcomed the unwelcomed, taught the disciples, touched the crippled, opened His heart to those who mourned, fasted, shared His food, was humiliated and abandoned by His friends, loved despite the painful rejection, was tortured, crucified and died upon a cross.

Yes, Jesus was humble.

"Jesus, meek and humble of heart, make my heart like unto Thine."

—Saint Thérèse of Lisieux

What a simple prayer it is to ask for humility.

There is no doubt that we all have a free will and can allow Jesus to love us or not. We have a choice to know Him, or just go about life as if He never existed. Many people do not want to hear the name of Jesus. You may risk losing your life in some places if you mention His name or refuse to deny Him. We could never count the martyrs who gave their lives for Jesus. We often ask for their prayers from heaven, because life is difficult for us here on earth. I think of Saint Teresa of Calcutta who suffered greatly, and worked tirelessly for the poor and dying. She did it all for Jesus.

The list could go on and on in regards to the saints who gave their lives for Jesus. Yet, it is so easy to forget Jesus, and go about our lives as if He were a figure from the past. He is real and wants so much to love us. He certainly knew the pain and suffering related to this world. He lived it more than you or I would even want to imagine.

I find the Parable of the Pharisee and the Tax Collector a great example of our own righteousness and the power of humility.

"He then addressed this parable to those who were convinced of their own righteousness and despised everyone else. Two people went up to the temple area to pray; one was a Pharisee and the other was a tax collector: The Pharisee took up his position and spoke this prayer to himself, 'O God, I thank you that I am not like the rest of humanity-greedy, dishonest, adulterous-or even like this tax collector. I fast twice a week, and I pay tithes on my whole income.' But the tax collector stood off at a distance and would not even raise his eyes to heaven but beat his breast and prayed, 'O God, be merciful to me, a sinner.' I tell you, the latter went home justified, not the former; for everyone who exalts himself will be humbled, and the one who humbles himself will be exalted."

—Luke 18:9-14

Reflection:

Will you be humble enough to allow Jesus to love you?

Be prepared for the blessings He will bring to your life. You will not be able to hold them within your heart. They will surely spill out and touch the lives of others too.

EPILOGUE

Years after retiring as a Kindergarten Teacher, I volunteered to help in a Preschool classroom. The children were four years old. Their teacher loved to teach them about Jesus. She told them to do kind things for others. This would make Jesus happy. Then you make room for Him so He can fill your heart with love. The simple messages are always the best.

I taught the children a simple prayer and told them it is only five words: "Jesus I trust in You."

This simple prayer is for us all, young and old. Jesus wants our trust so He can love us.

It may help you, as it helped me, to know that Jesus comes when there is a mess and not when we are perfect. A priest once told of how we clean our houses to get ready for a party. We may even hide things in the closet since we want everything neat and clean. We don't like people to see our bad side. We all want to look as if everything is just fine.

Jesus wants to come into the mess of our lives. We all have the mess. He wants to be with us and walk with us. He wants to heal us. Allow Jesus to love you.

ABOUT THE AUTHOR

Barbara Arbuckle is a retired Catholic school kindergarten teacher. She earned her bachelor's degree in elementary education from West Chester University. Barbara self-published a book entitled *Life Lessons from the Little Ones*. It is the words, wit and wisdom of the children. The children remind us of God's great love for us.

She, along with four other women, had a book published entitled *With God's Grace* in June, 2016. It is the mystery of God weaving together the lives of five strangers, and yet they share their personal healing and life-changing stories. They give glory to God for His abundant gift of grace in their lives.

She continues to write of her love for God, the Father, Jesus and the Holy Spirit. She honors and prays to Mary, our Blessed Mother.

She is blessed with a loving family: a husband of forty-seven years, a son, a daughter, a son-in-law and three precious grandsons.

REFERENCES

Scripture passages have been taken from:

The New American Bible, Revised Edition. Totowa, NJ: Catholic Book Publishing Corp., 2011.

Barbara Arbuckle, Sister Janice McGrane, SSJ, Elisa Taylor Berry, Arlene Finocchiaro, Annette Hug, (2016). With God's Grace Westbow Press, a Division of Thomas Nelson and Zondervan

Henri J.M. Nouwen, The Return of The Prodigal Son pgs. 42 and 114.

BIBLIOGRAPHY

Arbuckle, Barbara, Sister Janice McGrane, SSJ, Elisa Taylor Berry, Arlene Finocchiaro and Annette Hug. With God's Grace. Grand Rapids: WestBow Press, 2016.

Nouwen, Henri J.M. The Return of the Prodigal Son. New York: Doubleday, 1992.